LISTEN MY CHILD

Topics:

**Introduction.**

This book is dedicated to all parents, every child and counsellors who would want to use it to advise children accordingly to maintain the right character and family stability.

With the world changed and everyone on the job or business, counselling has lost value and morals are deteriorating at a higher rate than ever.

This means we are rising children without morals, respect and understanding of themselves.

Our old traditions, cultures, and values are all long gone due to the current conditions and the dot.com era. The only hope we still have are the old people who can guide us on the right way to behave and avail to us our history though this is also becoming complicated due to engagements and work of our parents and elders hence no time to pass on the message that they got from their parents.

I don't argue the fact that you have your own ambitions my child, your plans might be different from your parent's but what you must know, almost whatever you want to do has already existed or you want to modify what is there hence the need for more research on what is already there. This is a reason why parents and elders come into need since they have lived longer and have seen more of what you want to understand.

My child, the challenges you are facing, I experienced them that's why you should lend me your ears and heart for a moment so I can tell you all the tricks you require to sail through this world with ease, tricks and advice that I inherited from my elders who are long gone which made them successful and determined the legacy they left.

I know reading might be hard for you but try your best to finish and always refer to this book for comfort in case life becomes complicated. The things you see and the different wonders have always been triggered by what has ever existed because after all if nothing was worrying why would there be a need to find a solution?

I am partly what I am because of the mentorship of my elders, keep calm and learn my child you will not remain the same whatsoever.

**BACKGROUND AND THE FADING WORLD.**

My dear child, days are long gone since I was born and a lot has changed, I remember walking with my grandfather and most times, I would be with my parents and they told me riddles and parables, these were educative and I rilly had good time with them.

My father always taught me home duties and my mother was always there for me when my father would be harsh. My background is not so tight however if you compare it with today, a lot of differences are realised. The economy has changed to a man eat man society and everyone fights for him/herself and their family. This has widened the gap between parents and their children since most of them are always working till late to make their lives and their families better as jobs have replaced family time and parents now have less time with their children. This is eroding all the values and character in all societies around the globe.

I am blessed to pass on advice to you my child and would even be happier if you take it with one heart, practice it and pass it on to your children when you are grown up and with a family.

My dear child, the family I have sustained is largely because of values that my parents taught me and the relative's encouragement when my parent would be hard on me or when they were away.

Life was complicated in our days and the days of our ancestors; communication was hard and infrastructure was under developed. There was enough for survival and even neighbours were regarded as family members with many families in extended form.

Culture was still very strong and the rising of a child was a duty of every community member as I remember being asked a lot of questions by a stranger I didn't know when I delayed in town and he also disciplined me , in doing so he was doing what my parent was supposed to do. That's how we were brought up respecting all the people because we knew they had a right to punish us if we disrespected them like abusing or even refusing to greet them.

Misbehaving was a crime not only at home but also in the neighbourhood and this ofcos put fear in us and we would always live to their expectations and quarrelling with an elder was unheard of. This explains why we have strong friends unlike friendship of these days because you would pass through difficulties together. Education was difficult my child that's why most of my comrades are not educated however with this kind of upbringing we had, they are more than capable to manage their families than many educated fellows a reason why they are very successful and their children well educated.

These days its unheard of not to go to school, I took you to school the moment you reached three years old, now you have grown up and am entrusting you with these words. You spent much time with your teachers and less time with me. Even when you come from school for holiday, I take you for coaching because I want you to have better grades so you can have a better job and live a happy life. I have concentrated on developing your outside appearance and forgotten your inside which is your character yet it's the most treasured if you are to manage this world however, I believe after reading these words you will find it deep within you to forgive me for not giving you much attention and adopt these traits which you should then carry on to your children or young siblings. If you don't adopt these traits, you will not know what you are, will be taken up by different cultures, face different challenges and life will be complicated but if you sacrifice your time and learn them, you will live a satisfying life.

My old world is on the verge of disappearing with civilisation leaving the crawling and standing stage to running stage. Computers and technology are taking lead almost in every sector doing more than a half of the work efficiently and quickly. Life has become easier since there is a third-party technology which acts as a catalyser or fuel to speed up work and processes. You can now do almost everything with your phone at the comfort of your home ranging from ordering food, car to drive, workers and any other thing.

The new form of inequality looks like equality as everyone has access to internet and gadgets that's why a child of ten years has more computer knowledge than a fifty-year-old. I agree our old world was hard but it taught us to be strong and persevere in complicated situations or hardships. The current world makes everything seem easy that's why when the youth face challenges, they look for someone to criticise and blame because they are not used to hard life as its unusual to them.

Money is taking lead in almost every part of life and is becoming a new super power or a small god and without it no one values you at all. It has also created divisions and classes in all tribes and races. These days some people some people even kill for money as it's a super power they all want to possess. This was unheard of in our time my child because we valued more being human than being rich though these days some people say it's better to be very rich even for a short time than living along and satisfying life.

This brings a difference between our world and the new world and the new world. My dear child keep calm and learn because I want you to live a wealthy life and have morals. I am presenting you mistakes several people make that you can avoid, be wiser and confront several challenges with ease. This will give you a shortcut because you will stand on my mistakes and make right decisions. Your character matters a lot more than anything as 'you lose nothing when wealth goes, you lose something when health is lost and you lose everything when character is lost'.

Make yourself better and the world will admire you because you will be a source of inspiration and motivation to all people. There is no problem mending your own route but you will face challenges however, if you learn from the mistakes of others, you will start from their achievements and achieve more.

**THE GOLDEN HANDS.**

When I start writing about this, my head takes me back to the days I was a child. The person whose hands are blessed by God, whose care is incredible, whose love is immeasurable, whose guidance is key, whose sacrifice has no strings attached and has never lost trust in her child. I am talking about the mother's love. Respect your mother my child and don't ignore father's guidance.

On top of the nine months, my mother cared for me, she always protected me when I could not protect myself, she made sure everything was on my table and that I ate in time. I am proud your mother is doing the same my child.

She has protected you even when you are wrong, when you make a mistake it's her you tell first before I get to know and by the time, I know the situation is solved. She has sacrificed pleasures to get you the best you want. Even when there is no money, she fights harder, when am away she takes care so you don't miss your father makes you happy and you are her little angel and will always be even when old like I am to your grandmother.

She makes sure you don't lack or desire anything if she can afford it. When you wrong and I want to punish you, she complains on your behalf and tells you to change your behaviour in private. Though you may keep hurting her and you don't change, she still believes you can change. You ask her a lot of questions which she can't answer like;

Does my father love me?

Why don't you give what we ask for?

Why should I do what you want not what I want? And several others but she still calms you down.

When you wrong and exceed the limit, she punishes you with a few cains or simple slaps, you cry she picks you up. It's not that she hates you, she wants you to behave and be a valuable person in future. Times get complicated and you have the assignments, you sleep awake she makes coffee for you she is always close to you and wants you to feel her love.

When you succeed, she rejoices more than you and she feels happy, when you fail, she encourages you never to lose hope and to always focus so you can achieve. She does everything to help you overcome your challenges and she is the only one you can trust and feel confident.

When you grow up, she motivates you to be an important person with responsibility. She takes you to school and wants you to do law, engineering or medicine though you sometimes argue that you don't want them complaining that music, sports or business is your passion, she still forgets all she had said and encourages you to do what you want. When the whole family is against you doing that course you like, she is there to defend you. Her hands are soft and very strong as what she touches, she moves it. When you grow up, she opens to you and shows you the right way to behave, she teaches your sister how to handle a family when she is old. You are always a child in her eyes and sometimes she exceeds even when you are old and you feel angry but all she wants is to protect you more than anyone. When you start to understand, she teaches you how to behave in public and also how to manage a family. How blessed is your mother, doing all this expecting no pay right from waking up early to prepare you breakfast when you were a toddler up to now when you can do it yourself, visiting you at school and ensuring you are in good health when sick, she is sick too she stops all her activities to look after you, she gives you everything you ask for, how blessed you are the mother of my child.

Up to now, you have never paid her back and she still continues to care for you even when you disrespect her.  She asks you to pray to god when conditions are hard and teaches you to read the Bible (Holy books) on top of giving you verses of inspiration. Who else could bare that pain except your mother, even me your father I can't manage because it's a God given talent. Her golden hands don't harm, they raised you up to now, I know you may have disappointments with her and you may not like what she does in one way or the other but she is your mother and your only mother not replaceable. Her love for you is how you feel you would care for your child if you had only one.

When she quarrels listen to her, she is advising you how to cope up with the challenging world, if you quarrel back you are stubbing her in the neck and making her regret. When she punishes you, ask for forgiveness and learn from your mistakes. If she asks you to do your best, try as hard as possible and even when you fail, she will know you tried.

My child, replying your parents with a commanding voice while quarrelling is a sign of disrespect and you should desist from it as hard as possible. It brings sharp pain to the heart of your parent my child when you are advised to do what is right and you claim you are grown up and want liberty to make your decisions. You might not know they are angry because they don't want to show you that to you.

Some things you have done in the name of a mistake and have almost got your mother divorced but all those she doesn't consider because she sees your big picture when you are old. The more you hurt her not paying attention, the more she comes closer to you with more trust than before. A mother is just heaven sent; she cannot be replaced whatsoever.

Blessed are those who protect and rise children not of their own, how kind their hearts, they impact the right values in children on behalf of their parents who might be dead or alive but lost due to some reasons. My child I am glad me and your mother are still one however the other youth you interact with might not be having their parents but advise them not to be angry at them whatsoever as there could be strong reasons why they left them. Advise them to grant chance to any opportunity that allows them have their parents back because apparent can never be replaced no matter how hard they wronged you. If children die, you can produce others, if a partner dies you can get another one however if you lose your parent, you lose them forever you can never have them back or have substitute.

When you decide to start a business, it's the mother's ears with an interest to listen and she is the one who keeps sensitive secrets. When you win a gift and you are given money, it's the mother you inform. She is always eager to listen and ready to give you time when you need it. While going to school, your mother tops up on the pocket money I give you and she doesn't want me to know. All her money is spent on her dear children, when you do wrong, your mother is abused and blamed for poor upbringing, she takes the blame with one heart and tries to find a solution. How undisciplined you would be to disrespect your mother my child?

Now that you have grown up, fight for her, care for her and attend to her. In this way, she will rest a happy lady and give you all the blessings you need to succeed in life. A mother's achievements cannot be exhausted my child but we shall be basing on these as we continue the conversation. In our time, a mother always cared for her children until they began to understand. After that, she would concentrate on the daughter and grooming of the son would be the father's dear job.

## THE FATHER'S GREAT LOVE.

My child, I know I haven't given you all the time you need, care that you need and the care that you appreciate most. How I wish you would know the stress I pass through and the sleepless nights I spend just because of you. Every father's joy is seeing his children succeed and becoming responsible citizens. I know I have been hard and complicated for you and you are not free with me but in becoming hard, I fear that if I don't , you may not be successful and influential like I want or you would be stubborn yet I always want you to perform highly in everything you do.

I sometimes forget that you are a child and you need time to learn but I always calm down, listen to myself then and give you time to improve. My child I know I have not treated you equally in the family, I am hard on some and easy on others. When you were born and the way you grew up gave me away to treat you. The child who is hard hearted, I tend to be soft and provide everything they ask for. the one who grew up listening to me and doing everything I ask for, I become hard on them, this is because these are the ones whom I can entrust my property when I die so I keep testing until they are ready as they say pure gold has to be heated several times. If I have been hard on you my child it's because I trust you, I fear that if I make life easy for you, you might be arrogant and leave me with no one to trust. I am sorry but you have to allow me to do what am doing until you are ready as I was also treated the same way though I always thought my father hated me.

I thought he was not my real father and I even asked my mother why I was treated in the same way amidst the whole family. It was not until I was old and ready to marry that my father told me he always trusted me every minute of his life a reason why he made my life complicated so I could keep on track and be able to manage his property. This first challenged me ofcos, until I have produced you that I see a reason for not treating you like a king and I follow the same trend which I was made to pass through. Don't regard this hatred my dear child and though it might be hard on you, your father won't make the piece hard for you to swallow. There is no parent who can hate his children however, your father needs to be sure that you can manage his property when he is gone because he knows his success will turn to trash if he leaves no successor.

My dear child, don't envy your brother or sister when they are favoured most as these over burden your parents with complaints leaving them no option but to provide however, this should not make you inferior to your father or mother, if you lack anything, you have to be bold and ask for what you need. This world is full of in equalities, if you complain and demand for what you want, you get it. If you don't, others will because we all have same needs only that they come at different times to different people. Show a need and press for it until its fulfilled, don't be intimidated at any one point.

Your father is always working to ensure the family stands and is strong, he sleeps late, works for more hours just because he wants the family to be better one day and he ensures you don't lack anything. Sometimes he takes you to school because he wants to ensure you don't miss him, he takes loans to facilitate the family or business and he makes sure you are always on the same level with other children in the neighbourhood.

Even when you fall sick, he makes sure you are in the best hospital of his choice. Never under estimate the efforts of your father my child, if he encourages you inform of quarrelling, don't trouble him, allow what he says and even if it's unfair don't complain right away, leave him to calm down and then ask him politely or ask your mother to help you my child because she has the power to influence him at any one point even when he sworn heaven on earth not to do something, he can change with the influence of your mother. Avoid direct confrontation of your father as it's a sign of dis respect. My dear child, I love you and your mother loves you however if you see that we have a simple misunderstanding, please never show your side even when you are old. Even when am wrong or your mother is wrong, never enter a misunderstanding if you want your family to remain intact. Just keep quiet and only help if it necessitates but even after, don't show aside please as this can facilitate divorce after the defeated parent knows that children are against him/her. Desist from that my child or advise your friend accordingly if in similar situation.

You have to understand that we live in a world of economics and scarcity applies to every one of us that's why I can't provide everything you ask for as it's not possible and even your neds cannot be fulfilled once in one day, the more you grow the more your needs increase since they are insatiable and uncountable.

If you ask ten things and I give you one, you should appreciate because this gives me morale to provide bigger things, it brings joy to my heart, lets me criticise myself why I don't buy at least a half of your requests so I can increase my trust in you. If you reject what you are given from your parent, it demoralises them and they always hate whatever you ask for and they always quarrel before they provide its just because they hate your character and wouldn't want to make you happy even if they don't tell you. You should learn to appreciate everything you get or what you have my child because you are a step ahead of majority who are seriously wanting.

Learning to have a satisfied heart gives you ground where you base to make improvements and push harder as it helps you value yourself, understand your cause and shows you a reason why you should improve. This also rises your status in society because all people want to be applauded for every achievement they make, so you will be a darling and many will always want to associate with you. My dear child even though I have wronged you several times and seemed as if I don't care , I am humbly sorry and please take on my advice and find a place in your heart to forgive your father but also press me harder if you want something and even if I complain, I will take the message.

You also have to understand my child that you are young and you need my advice to make a decision. Your age might tell you that a decision you are making is right and if I don't guide you now you will regret that your father did nothing my child. That's why you have to believe me and entrust me with your life because I have never wished you anything in appropriate.

Even when you feel conditions are hard, never take a decision to escape from home my child, we all saw difficulties and I may not be the best parent but I have never wished to see my child leave me. This proves you are weak and also demoralises you because this world is so complicated like swallowing a pair of razorblades and if you can't manage or learn to live with your own father(parent) then how will you manage people you don't know. This is why you must be stronger than ever before and focus on what is important to you as you respect your parent. My child, as you grow you will find several advisers in different arenas and some will seem more important than your own father but not all are meant to be trusted. Listen to them but never let anyone take a place of your father, trust very few of them.

Try as hard as possible to learn every day and challenge yourself with new content and new information if you want to be influential. Train yourself to learn new habits that will make you because it's the habit you develop that makes you the kind of person you become. Some of these habits are reading, dealing with people, good feeding and several others. Don't learn bad habits such as taking drugs or alcoholism because such will destroy you and you will live a life of regrets.

My child can you produce your own child and then you hate him/her? the same way you would feel for your child your own blood is the same way I feel for you that's why I sacrifice everything to make your life better. Do what you are supposed to do and I will do my part but never lose your focus.

Mind the kind of people you come nearer to, appreciate your relatives but understand what they say before they give you help. If its building you and your family, trust them the more however if they want your family to dis integrate or they are against one of your parents then you have to open your eyes because they may be sowing a poisonous seed in you. Let's find out more about our relatives in the next lesson.

## THE HELPING HAND.

As you grow my child, you will realise many hands giving you support. Some are the people you know and others are the strangers that you have never seen. Your relatives are of a great value and never under estimate their efforts however small it may be, they should be your inspiration and you should learn from them my child because they know what our culture means. The current situation doesn't allow to know all your relatives but at least fight to know all those close to your family because they are part of you and they are your immediate contacts for help in any situation. How great the value of advice from a paternal uncle and aunt is? they give you straight forward advice that helps you focus and achieve. They will appreciate and love you in all situation though they don't easily show this. They want you to focus and succeed that's why they may be hard to deal with or may not be so close to you my child but you must trust them because they want your father's blood and can never let you down. Focus on your aim and they will support you with all they can and all you children are your sisters and brothers having any of them in an affair is incest. Please don't do this my child, there are other better people outside than your own blood and incest is also a sin in the eyes of God.

The maternal relatives are always incredible, they contribution is always invaluable they always fight to make their sister's child better and they give all the care you might need. They will keep your secrets if you entrust them or if you want to start a project, they value you and may even be willing to support you with everything including money and advice. They will protect you and show you the good care, do for you whatever you ask for and encourage you to work harder. However, you must be keen to take their advice so they don't divert you from your family values.

My child, if there is a conflict between your relatives, please don't show aside and respect all of them and treat them equally without favouring any. This will earn you support from all sides and you will gain more as you continue to respect all sides, maybe you might be a reason for their uniting again.

When conditions are tough, the relatives are available to give you guidance, some have attained higher positions in different sectors and are ready to give you a helping hand when you prove yourself worth. At school, you study from town and they are there to take good care of you when you approach them. Learn to appreciate your relatives my child. Never assume it's their responsibility to take care of you and even if it may be, you lose nothing thanking them or even surprising them with petty gifts which are very cheap but there is everything to gain when you do it. My child, I understand some of your relatives are in high position in government or even in the business sector but that is not enough to guarantee you a job or privileges, you have to go an extra step and befriend them on a personal basis. To do this, you must stand out and prove to them that you know what you want and mean it. Ask for their advice instead of material things, this will draw them closer to you and they will trust you the more. Never make an error of the current youth of asking for money or presenting requests to be fulfilled to such distinguished people. They may give you the money but they will not value you hence this means you are sacrificing and enjoying pleasures today at the expense of tomorrow, yet if you asked for advice there would be a possibility of getting both the money and the advice.

Advice is key my child because it brings understanding and wisdom. This is better than every possession of man, with it you achieve all the riches and wealth you would ever need, become more successful and more influential. That's why its better to teach a person how to fish than give them free fish, teach how to make money than give free money and teach them how to be successful than making them your successor. All this is done by wisdom my child, that's why I am encouraging you to always learn and devise a lesson from every situation you face. The helping hand can also be strangers. These are people you have never seen but because you stand out, they are always ready to give you help. Consider walking in away with several friends and someone comes running at ahigh speed, what would you do? you would all create way for that person to pass. The same applies when you are focussed and you know what you want. those who don't know you would create away for you away and wish you the best, however what would happen if you all stood aside and you saw the person stop where you are or a few metres in front of you, how would you feel ?, the immediate question would be what is this one up to and why was he/she running in the first place?. You would even feel angry for the person so in the same way if you show people that you are focussed and you stagger along the way, then they would feel more bitter than in the first place. This is a reason why you should always stand to every decision you make.

There are influential people you will meet on the way as you try to achieve your dreams. These are your network, never let them go pay more attention to their advice and they will always feel safe with you, take you to their homes and entrust you with their businesses. Never be greedy, always try to fulfil what they entrust you with my child and life will be easy for you. It feels good to achieve at a young age and become a celebrity however, this is sometimes impossible because of scarcity and the condition but keep calm and focussed, your time will come my child and when you are ready you will get everything you want.

Don't over love money it's not everything my child, know what to do for money and what you shouldn't do for money. This will reserve your respect in people and they will know you are invaluable. The love for money is the root of all evil, but having money is actually the best thing. Money acts as fuel to fulfil your dream so if you can learn to live with it and without it then it will not control you and you will manage this world. Your siblings respect you my child, they respect you next to your parents and this puts a lot of responsibility on your shoulders which you should serve with one heart. You are the next in my shoes that's why I am telling you all this and equipping you with relevant skills to be outstanding in every field you undertake.

Never argue with your siblings or your family when they want you to do or handle all the work instead appreciate their trust and never let them down. When I was young, my father used to give me a lot of work and sometimes I hated it, I would argue why my father entrusted me with all the work yet I wasn't even the first born. It was one day when I met my maternal uncle who had also been to that same position and he encouraged me to always appreciate responsibilities however many they would be and because he was one of my mentors, then I was rilly touched and I easily started handling them. The more I handle, the sharper I become and the more focussed I be.

So, my child allow all the responsibilities the way they come and look for means to handle them as this trains you for the important person that you would become. There is no punishment if you ask, it's understandable that you may not know everything my child, if you ask you will get to know better than keeping quiet and repeating the mistakes that you can avoid when you ask for guidance.

When you have grown up and people entrust you with a certain position to lead them, never let them down. Lead them without fear or favour, protect the disadvantaged my child and don't cheat the poor when you are in position to serve them because God protects them, give them what belongs to them and your father in heaven will bless you. When you are aging and you are made a government official, never eat the money of the tax collectors. Corruption is a bad vice, take what belongs to you and your father in heaven will give you the wisdom to multiply it and become wealthier. When you steal government funds, you can build a house, start a business or even go on a vacation but the cries of the people can never allow you enjoy that money. You will live with

self-judgement as every day it turns from worse to worst. Your behaviour changes and you can no longer trust anyone because you look at them as your enemies and you think they are going to judge you.

It's not true my child that to be rich and even build a house on more than an acre of land or have very many businesses and workers, you have to steal. You can learn how to do all this and God will guide you to the kind of riches you want. Wealth is good but wealth without character, better it never existed because it only grooms a monster. So, never attract a curse on yourself and family by stealing government funds when you are in position to serve people. Serve people well and they will praise you, make you a hero and write you in the books of records. This will create good reputation my child and everywhere your family goes they will be warmly welcomed. This is why I have tried to be fair to all and treated all people equally so that wherever you go and introduce yourself as my child, you will be given a warm welcome.

Pay attention to your teachers my child, these have been trained to handle you at all levels and occupy the place of a parent. Much of your time is spent at school and so they are your immediate help in case of any emergency. Disrespecting your teacher is equal to disrespecting me and if I am informed, I will punish you myself. Consult them in all fields, fight harder to get knowledge from them, ask a lot of relevant questions and task them to get you Up to Date material content. The good thing is that these are eager and more than willing to offer help though students are not interested in them. Use every chance when it's still available, don't try to copy others and be yourself at the end of your youth age, you will count yourself lucky as you remember this advice. Some opportunities are seasonal, you should learn and take advantage of them or else they will disappear for good. More so, use a person's services when they can still avail them to you freely hence it requires a lot of discipline to understand and use what you are given. My child, everyone can say they understand how to use what they are given but most times opportunities appear at a time when you can't easily determine them or at your weakest point. That's why I am over emphasizing self-discipline as hard as possible.

My dear child, the helping hand will always be available but most times if you are not strategic, then you might not be able to realise it and you will always blame everyone and for every condition you face. The magic hand can be available however, the more it avails, the more the need to solve greater challenges and remember majority have their trust in you so you can't let them down.

**DEALING WITH CHALLENGES.**

My child its true you will face several challenges but learning to handle every challenge as it appears is key. These start from home when you start to understand and you realise you are treated unfairly or you don't get everything you ask for like your siblings. from here you go to school where you find students with different character and they bully you, the teachers may also be segregative or even the administration. The family enemies will never want to see you succeed, they fight everything you put up such as a business or even when you excel at school it becomes a crime since all your cousins become jealousy.

They leave you all the work alone right from home, to school, to even work place when you get a per time job. Adolescence also comes in with its other challenges which you may not be free to share with friends or family. This makes life complicated to fulfil all the demands and responsibilities you may have from different sides parents, school, friend and life. My dear child all this should not break you, I have written to prepare you to confront all these challenges and not miss even a single of them because some come with hidden opportunities.

My daughter your challenges are broad and some you don't bring them yourself. I know the adolescence stage affects you most and you have your own personal desires which you don't want your parent to know but this is not good my child. if you rilly feel you have something urgent and you fear confronting them, please write it down and drop it on my bed or my table where I can't fail to see it or if that doesn't work, then use a relative or your close friend to tell me; it could even be your school councillor or family friend. When you don't do this, there are monsters out there who take advantage of every situation hence will be ready to give you anything you want on a condition of harassing you sexually. This not only affects you mentally but also physically and you may hate yourself or contract the disease so my daughter please, never receive gifts you don't know and be keen the people you relate with my dear even your own classmates might be in illegal businesses such as human trafficking, bad character has no age don't trust anyone because you think they are so young for illegal activities. Be with them but don't let them come closer to you and know everything about you.

I am telling you all this because I have seen it with my bare eyes, and my friends became victims in similar circumstances. No one loves you more than your own parent as I said earlier, if you produced, who would love your, child more than you? ofcos no one. This is the same love I have for you. Mind your dressing my daughter because sometimes it calls a lot of attention to you which you may not need. Dress decently and even the harassers will fear approaching you since you don't incite them anymore and you get more respected.

Being famous doesn't mean you are respected, keep calm and don't attract attention and you will get the best partner you want for the future as all people respect you for what you are. The Bible says resist the devil and he will flee from you so please never be intimidated. Keep focussed and you will access all that you want. Just give it time, though if you rush for worldly desires you will live a regretful life.

There are some challenges which you don't know their where abouts my child, but you don't have to fear all you have to do is be strong and not be shaken. My dear son, I know you face a lot of difficulties which you can't tell anyone about, you admire a lot , you want your own car, your own house at a younger age and you fear telling anyone because they will tell you to wait for your time. You always want to help when you don't see anyone in need but you don't have the money to help them, you feel you have grown up and you need your own business, want to feel important, have a lot of money and live an easy life and all this is coupled with the many responsibilities that might be on your shoulders. This can bring a delusion in your head in your head and you start thinking you are too late to start working or to get rich. I have been through all this that's why I am telling you, I was even very desperate to make money and run my own business to the extent that I couldn't allow to sleep, I always wanted to find out which is the easiest way to make money. All this is understandable my child, it's okay to be desperate but don't let your high ambitions exceed your mission and goal. You can achieve everything and be anyone as long as you give it time. I am not saying you can't break a world record but you also have to consider other factors. Don't expect to become a president at 18years when you have just adopted that idea at 16years of age. It's impossible to achieve such an aim in two years but you can achieve it at 40 or 50 years if you are determined. So, every ambition you have should be given realistic time and if you do your part well, then all odds are in your favour.

There is no free lunch my child, no one should lie to you that they are giving you a favour unless it is your parent. Actually, even parents expect a return when they give you anything for example if your parent buys you a gift, they expect more love, respect and improvement in your grades in return as an exchange for the gift. If apparent can do something for you in good faith and still expects a return, how much more would a stranger or just a relative expect when they do anything for you. Though they may tell you that the deal is totally, don't rush to accept it not all that glitters is gold. More so there is no short cut to wealth or success and if you try to take hasty shortcuts, you may regret for the rest of your life even wealth created tends to have no background and it disappears quickly since it lucks a pillar. What would it profit you to become rich for a year or two driving Porsche cars and in the most expensive house then you restart your total misery after that? Don't you think life would be more frustrating than in the first place?

I am not saying there are no get rich quick schemes either but most of them will bring you trouble. If you rilly want to get rich quickly my child then you have to get ready to take all the steps, overturn all the stones and in the shortest time. This will require a lot of your sacrifice, sleepless nights, more research, more reading, more hunger, more risks, more learning, more network and more discipline with commitment. This is the shortest way to wealth if you can manage it then you will be very rich in a very short time such as five years but if you can't, keep calm and take every step as it appears. This can take you up to 20years or more but the stress is not a lot since its distributed along that time. So, it's up to you my child whichever way you take if you are faithful you will make it, however if you take a wrong way in the name of being quick then you might regret the decision day, I hope you listen to me on this.

Avoid joining peer groups at school my child, some may add value on you but many are more poisonous. Remember you all come from different homes and backgrounds which signifies you have different characters and behaviours. This is the truth but when you are together you try to live on the same standards which means if you are not able to influence them to live by your values then you will live by their standards and when this happens you forget your former self. I am now old my child, I saw then and I continue to see children with good character being spoilt by bad peer groups and when this happens, they totally hate themselves when they are back to their senses or they are spoilt forever. These groups will teach you poor habits such as drug abuse, alcoholism, disrespect and many others which affects not only your health and wealth but also pushes your friends away from you.

Not all groups are bad however but whatever group that does something which you think if done to you makes you uncomfortable, then its better you don't come closer to it. If you are teased or bullied my child keep strong, report to relevant authorities and don't try to revenge as you will also look like them. Silence doesn't mean that you are a fool, it simply means you understand better than your opponent so just keep quiet and let them talk or say whatever they want. Ignore them and keep living by your standards my child and at one point they will realise they are losers and will come to join you. Allow them but keep alert.

Don't be intimidated by your haters because you are a step ahead of them and also never get angry for too long as this makes you a slave of them. Keep focussed, fight in silence and they will always be the first ones to recognise your results and success. Keep achieving and they will soon realise they are running after God's own child because the more they hate, the more you will succeed. If things get tough, get more determined, if the road gets rough then change the shoes but don't be diverted or quit because you can't know when the opportunity for your breakthrough will appear.

Challenges must come but the decision you take will either set you free or bound you up. Most of the time, keep your eyes open my child because you may attract problems to yourself in the name of comfort, easy friends, chance, enjoyment and several others so never make a decision without thinking twice.

## THE DOT.COM ERA.

The world has become a global village with almost similar issues, problems and solutions my child. Internet has connected the whole world, technology has done amazing things and made work easier for everyone. Right from the food you eat on which boosters are applied in the garden, the clothes you wear, the phone you use, the house you sleep in, the ride we use, the electricity and literally everything. All this has been discovered by people who are ambitious and dreamt of having a better world and at the end they succeeded in almost every aspect. The dot.com era has brought positive effects but never the less, the negatives are also accumulating. At my age, we are holding the same age type and you even have a better brand than mine. You know all the functions that I don't know and this equates us since we all get the same information hence your level of understanding is way beyond mine. You can use your phone to do anything you want such as running online businesses, making connections and getting different information that you require in any situation.

No one limits you to use your phone my child, that gadget can build your life if you use it profitably or destroy it completely. The world has gone wild and they post everything on internet including pornographic photos and videos. These do not only destroy your mental capacity but also ruins your character and leads to addiction. This will ruin your relations with your opposite sex friends because you will always see them as moving sex instruments. This means you will not be able to work with them in any situation and when they know it, some of them can take advantage of your weakness and influence you to make poor decisions. More so, spiritually its disastrous since it negatively affects your relations with your God and morally it's also ashaming especially if anyone finds out. It also stimulates growth of weird characters such as masturbation, lesbianism and homosexuality so please my child desist from watching this material if you have been watching.

On internet and different platforms, you can also learn different habits that may shape your character but it's not a must that whatever you see you have to try it my child. Different selfish people chasing their hidden interests might encourage you that some characters are better than many but that's a lie, please try to limit yourself from learning anew habit if it's not from your home. This doesn't stop you from learning developmental habits that usually pay a lot in the long run. Actually, if you are keen, you will draw a line of difference between these habits. Mostly, easy to learn habits are always bad ones the right habits need consistency and are hard to learn, they require extra efforts and persistence for example reading, waking up early, marketing, decision making and others. These hard to learn habits will add value on you and will improve your home so sacrifice to learn them. In our days, phones were not common and in the days of our ancestors, they were using ancestors as there were no phones. The world is becoming easier and a better place to live in but only for the intelligent and if you can understand the advantages coming with the dot.com era and use them, then trust me, you will be looked up as a pool of wisdom and everyone will always come to you for advice. It's not that people who mess up and are losers have never heard constructive words my child as this is a very large group and some of them were once very intelligent.

Those who were over ambitious, messed up and lost out forever in life, those who heard and ignored thinking it's all a lie, and the dis advantaged group which has never heard anything however these have a chance of changing if they realise the information and try to change. Becoming rich is good however if you are still young in school, no matter high you are motivated, don't try to leave school and start a business. You should first finish a level such as high school for you to take such a hard decision because if you quit before you are old, you might mess up and end up a loser no matter how creative you might mess up and end up a loser no matter how creative you might be because when you take such a decision pre maturely, your parents might ignore you forever. So always think twice before you can take such a hard decision as Africans say, never bite a hand that feeds you.

With dot.com era, you can keep in your house and everything is delivered to you for example you can work from home hence no need to visit the work place, order for a nice phone from home, nice clothes or even food and everything is delivered on your door, you are paid on your phone, you pay all bills with your phone which seems enjoyable and easy however this has increased laziness to its highest level a reason why fitness coaches have emerged and are paid a lot, and some people have even made it a profession. It has also increased heart related diseases, blood pressure, obesity and several others. These were very few in our days since you would walk to the work place or ride hence in the process you would exercise. So, my child learn to spare some time for exercise because it is good for your health. A lot has been put in place to distract young brains my child, the television programmes, the different games not only on phone but also on computers , all these take your attention and a lot of your time they enslave you and unless you open up your mind and take this advice, you will keep a slave. I know you always want to watch cartoons, music and other entertaining programmes though I sometimes interfere to put different programmes or even news.

Now remember the people you are watching, did their best trained and prepared to put something entertaining so if you keep watching, what do you gain or what will you leave for others to watch or learn from you when you are gone. I should have put a rule that 'NO WATCHING TV UNTILL YOU DO SOMETHING OF VALUE EVERY DAY' but I feared you would hate me as your minds were still young, now that you are old please follow it yourself and the results will be amazing trust me. Since almost no one is after you in this dot.com era, you must be your own coach my dear child and be a hard coach to yourself. Always set high limits and break them then set higher limits, learn the right way to relate to people, greeting, approach, and how you can be more creative than you have been. Learn to manage yourself well and balance your time among the different activities you may want to do such as reading, social media, entertainment, learning anew skill or practicing, visiting a friend and any other that you may want to do. Don't allow to be addicted to anything my child, learn to divert your attention when it necessitates because when you are addicted, you become a slave as you are like a goat, tied with a rope around its neck to a peg hence what you are addicted to will influence you always and you won't make any independent decisions.

Every time you are watching a television show, make sure there is something of value that is added on you and in so doing you will get the best out of everything, and if your eyes are open, opportunities will always show themselves to you. My child your parents might delay at work and you are left home alone, you have to do something of value with your life and don't wait for them to first complain. If you want anything in life you must toil and work harder for it, it's not always your parents concerned because very soon, they will send you a way to start your own home and if you never prepared then it will be a tag of war for you that's why you must be a hard coach to yourself and never feel sorry if you are doing anything. Don't allow a lot of grace for people who might feel concerned about you. Keep focussed and hustling, relatives and friends might try to discourage you asking you why you are punishing yourself and doing a lot of work but always ask them, would you allow to be punished by the world or you would rather punish yourself earlier before the world starts to so that by the time it tries you are stabilised already?

The dot.com era has improved technology which is your chance to be innovative and creative. Don't wait for others to create everything, develop a sixth sense of intuitiveness and be on the lookout, everything you buy or you hold ask yourself these three questions;

1.  How was this made?

2.   How do I improve it?
3.   What do I need to do it?

If the above three questions are answered well, then they will lead you to the right people you should consult and the resources you need then you will base on that to improve the product. If you can't do that, then lookout for the needs of people, make research and try to solve their problems and in so doing you will discover new things that have not existed before. These are the advantages that come along with civilisation and the dot.com era as when the right information is exposed to young and fresh minds, they are able to think over it, create and innovate products respectively. This is a reason why most discoveries these days are done by young people. In this struggle don't be left behind my child, open your eyes wide and desire more, creativity has no age, you must do something they will always remember you for and that adds value on people's lives.

As they say if you want good history and remembrance, write it about yourself hence make people's lives better and you will always be their favourite and many will name their children by your name and your innovations. With this dot.com era and technology, this is very easy. All in all appreciate this era my child as life has become easier however open your eyes widely and take advantage of every opportunity, don't be taken up by dot.com as it can divert you since it has a lot to distract your attention and when you have respected these principles well, you will appreciate the satisfying life that you will have lived even in your old age as you pass on this small book to your child.

In everything you are doing, you will have to deal with people my child that's why you should know which kinds of people to work with.

## CHOOSING FRIENDS.

My dear child, pay attention to this topic because when you learn it well, it can influence all the others. Choosing a trusted friend is one of the most complicated challenges that has ever existed. This is because the person whom you see they deserve your trust is the same who does something unpredictable the next day and you start regretting how hard you trusted them. A person's close friend shares more than 50% of a person's character because when they live together, they start practicing everything together and as one hence in the end they all acquire similar characteristics. This is a reason why you should be keen when choosing a friend and be selective on the people you allow near you as they have a lot of impact on you.

As we start this conversation, before we finish you should be able to make friends with a difference. A trusted friend is the one whom you can easily recommend to describe your character or behaviour and you trust them to give the right information about you. There are three categories of people from whom you can select a friend.

1. Better than you.
2. Same level as you.
3. Lower than you.

From these, you are to selectively choose a friend(s) with whom you share ideas.

Those better than you are a step ahead of you in ideas, family background, age or skills. This is the first category of people that you must select in. when you befriend this category, you get the knowledge and the skills they have or if their families are well off and known then you get connection and network. You can also develop your ideas with the help of these as they may have the capital that they want to invest. This group deserves your respect, never let them down and whenever dealing with them, pay attention to them and listen attentively. They may have ideas but lack courage and the technical know-how which you can give them and you work together. This group is amine of diamond and it's not easy to approach or win their trust however if you do, they tend to over trust you.

The second category is those whom you are at the same level, these have the same ideas like you, are better than you in one thing and you are better than them in another, they are always eager to learn and when they approach you  they ask specific and relevant questions and they always feel safe being around you as you both think alike. With these, you can develop one another if you join hands and both of you open your third eye. These have different categories also but make sure you chose the one who has a skill you don't have but related in your field of work so you can learn from one another. These can be related to a mine of gold since they are available though in small numbers and when you get them, you can't afford to let them go. Hold on to them, respect them as they respect you back and work together to achieve your dreams.

The third category are the ones lower than you. Some may be focused and trying, others in their own ignorant life and others may be in need of your help. In this group, you don't have to befriend majority people because many don't know what they want and they might divert you if you come closer to them.

My child, try by all means not to associate with the disadvantaged or the unlucky. These are people who are ever complaining and they are never bothered to find out a solution for their problems. If you must help them use a third party or keep them far from you because if you bring them closer in the name of helping they still will always complain because it's part of them, their complaints will feel your head and affect your thinking hence you miss to do what you are supposed to do, regret your time wasted and also join them to complain. That's why I am saying, never even come closer to them as they are like poisonous snakes.

In this third category, you will choose very few who are focussed and the rest you ignore however you have to learn how to deal with all people. I am saying you choose in all the three groups because the first category gives you ideas, the second category are your partners or stake holders and the third category are your workers that's why you need to choose in all the categories however you have to be keen. Treat all these people in their categories and the way they are so they don't know what you want as you use them in fulfilment of your dreams. Learn to know the character of the person you want to make your friend. This is a bit complicated but if you can know their character, they will be easy for you to work with. Just give it time and don't be strict, you will find out what they love to do most without supervision. The more you observe them, the more it becomes easier for you to discover their character and if they have a habit that is hard to live with, keep them at an arm's length as you advise accordingly. Know all the details about your friend my child, somethings might seem normal such as not asking about the parents of your friend but they are not right. When I was schooling, I had my best friend John (RIP) whom we shared almost everything and our traits were almost the same since we shared more than 60% of each other's life. God decided and he left me at a young age and guess what, I never knew his family and he never knew mine, I had to start looking for directions to a home I had never visited before, my friends would also ask me his father's name and I could not know. This hurt me so much, added shame on misery and taught me a lesson I will never forget. If you are very close to a person, avail them part of the essential information such as home address, parents' names and others and also take the initiative to ask even if they are not interested. This can help trace a person in case of anything and more so, it builds a bond of trust. If your friend cannot tell you the details of their home and parents, its better you leave them or keep an arm's length. If they avail you these details, Introduce them to your parents or ask for a home visit. This will build trust and there is nothing to worry about because you know them more.

If the families know each other and the person is your close friend, then you can easily recommend them to represent you or describe you. At school, do not segregate yourself and have a few friends my child, befriend all people and be sure to treat them the way everyone comes but trust very few this is because you come up with a product or idea, it can be easy for you turn these friends into customers however you may not need to join you to start accompany. It's possible to befriend more than ten thousand people and you trust only two of them. So, you must learn that trick by being free to everyone. Resilience and persistence are key, you should monitor how the person behaves especially when faced with a problem or in a crisis because if you don't find out this early then it might be difficult for you in the hard times since you might be alone in confronting the problem.

You may not be assured that you will get someone who is totally pure, NO!! however if you can manage to live with their weakness, can easily influence them or motivate them, then you take the decision to bring them closer because when you are two and are faced with a problem or hinderance, you can easily persevere through it than when you are one as the English say ' Two heads are better than one' so it's crucial to have a friend. My child, as we finish this topic, never force yourself on any person at any time. If the person was not meant to be your friend they cannot be and also, never value friendship for material or quick gains especially for your opposite sex friends. In whatever transaction or business that you include a friend ensure it's a win! win! When you do all this, you will get the friends of value whom you can easily work together.

## TAKING DECISIONS.

My child, decision making is one of the most important traits that is taught almost nowhere. In schools, they don't teach you how to make a decision especially when the condition is difficult but thank God, I learnt this trait and I am handing it over to you. Most times, deciding is always difficult for majority people due to;

- ✓ Fear of making a mistake
- ✓ Fear of being criticised
- ✓ Ignorance about the subject matter
- ✓ Similarity of events.

All these fears are strong forces which limit and scare people from taking decisions easily and quickly.

Fear of making a mistake.

Because of the education system which bring up students hating failure, even in life people fear to take decisions due to fear that they may make mistakes however this is not the case because every successful person who exists appreciates failure as a source of learning. The people who designed the education system wanted to instil fear in majority people so that they do not try out different values, this is in the end was to reduce competition and it has been achieved so if you rilly want to succeed in life and become influential, you will need to un learn some of the negative traits embedded in your head so you can be set free.

Failure is simply feedback from the market, it simply means you have to upgrade your product quality, efficiency and effectiveness. The quicker you listen to failure and take action, the better the results, the quicker the absorption of your product hence without failure there is no urge to improve, no room for creativity and innovation and no improvement in the quality of a product. Failure is also an opportunity to start again and avoid errors so appreciate failure and don't fear mistakes because they are a source of learning and the more you learn the more the experience which helps you in day to day experiments(your ventures) for you to determine your future expectations(your goals& dreams). So, in making a decision, never fear making a mistake because they are necessary if you are to succeed.

Fear of being criticised.

Many people actually fear criticism arising from making a wrong decision hence they delay or never make a decision at all. To you my child, you should learn to accept criticism as it's a source of learning and part of it, is actually feedback. What would it profit you to ignore making a decision in favour of fear and you leave your work undone? how would you know that people are with you or against you if you never want to hear criticism? Self-discipline is key my child, if you can manage people's talk and you still remain calm, life will be easy for you. People must always criticise whether you do something or you don't so better make the decision if it's wrong, you will learn and if its right you will appreciate yourself.

Ignorance about the subject matter.

Some people don't actually know much about the subject matter, many administrators or even students do not make decisions because they don't know much about the subject. They over delegate their work to others and when a crucial decision is to be taken, they don't know where to start from. This is brought about by mis management and laziness by those in authority. My child, never assume everything is right when it's not and allowing incomplete information or basing on it to make a decision is suicidal. Always be on the lookout and in control of everything you are entitled to and get more information concerning the things that you have direct or indirect control over. This will aid in making a quick decision than trying to gather all the necessary information at the last minute.

Similarity of events.

There are situations which look alike and this makes decision making difficult. You can't tell what is right or what is wrong hence a complicated situation is created where making a decision is difficult since all situations are confusing. More so the decision might be so difficult that if you make a mistake, it comes with very heavy costs hence scares people from even trying. My child I am telling you reasons why people don't make decisions quickly so that if you are in a similar situation, you take relevant measures. I always enjoy stories of hunters: whenever they would go to hunt in the forest, they would not know where the animals were but, in the forest, they would throw a stone or a stick in the bush to see what comes out, and out of the ten bushes they try, at least in one they would find an animal and the meal for the day would be covered. You can adopt this also, if you take a decision, it has two sides success and failure hence you are entitled to any of the two however if you don't take a decision, failure is inevitable. So why not try your chance and if you can gather relevant information and has done research, why hesitate? Take the decision and you will learn along the way whether to make necessary amendments or not.

In decision making you have to understand all the sides, there are times when you have to choose the 'necessary' and ignore the 'important', survival and pleasure cannot be equated though they may both be in the same category. There are events and engagements that are important but not necessary and if you follow them, you might be misled. For example, attending a birth day party for your close friend or sister when you have an exam the next day would not be a good decision.   Below is a way to differentiate the necessary things from important things.

Necessary;

- ✓ Come once in a long period
- ✓ Very high costs if missed
- ✓ Ruins your life and dreams
- ✓ Have a long-term impact
- ✓ Might seem less important some times
- ✓ Require personal supervision
- ✓ Can cause death or suicide

Important;

- ✓ Always appear
- ✓ Costs are minimal if missed
- ✓ Ruins friendship if missed
- ✓ Have a short-term impact

✓ Can be highly advertised as very important
✓ It's possible to delegate them
✓ Can cause depression or illness but not death

These and several other differences explain the necessary things from essential things. Examples include;

Necessary:

- End of year examination
- Immediate accident
- Sick friend or relative in intensive care.
- Attending to a complaining customer
- A business meeting when you are chairman or main speaker.

Important:

- Birthday party
- Outing with friends
- Porsche cars
- Honey moon with loved ones.
- Visiting expensive hotels or visiting friends, etc

The above can be important or necessary depending on which situation and what you are comparing it with.

So in making a decision, if it can cause death of life take it, if it ruins friendship and is not necessary, leave it, if it's in line with your main goals and dreams, no matter how complicated the situation might seem, take it immediately, if its urgent and important but not necessary, leave it, if you can't manage the outcome costs of its negativity, leave it, if it's not clear, leave it, if it has all the relevant details, take it, etc. So, take a decision without any emotions my child because emotions usually lead to making of wrong decisions. In making a decision, do not focus on the obstacles along the way but focus on the final outcome or product. Ensure you have all the necessary efforts to work on the decision before you take it. This doesn't mean having all the requirements but the main without which you can't start on the venture.

Ensure time management in decision making as too early and you make mistakes, too late and you incur a lot of costs, so make sure you make a decision at the right time my child and you can't do this if you are not keen or if you don't think twice before you act. Don't panic in making any decision as panic comes with its consequences, FEAR is just False Evidence Appearing Real so don't be intimidated by what you can't see.

## THE FUTURE PREPARATION.

I see it wise to advise you on this topic though I see it far from your sight. If you are not having this knowledge you might mess up and regret yet I have the medicine hence it would be unfair not telling you. Fore warned is fore armed hence open your eyes and ears to this message. The kind of partner you choose determines the friends you will keep with, the children you produce, the life you live and if they are cooperative also determine the level of wealth you reach.

I know that you have heard several quotes about this topic like 'Behind every successful man is a strong woman' and 'Behind every successful lady is a supportive man' and many others. These are true but actually, some people can't explain why and it's all explained by the power of love. Love can move mountains, in the first quote, don't think that the lady actually does work but the love, care and trust she provides to the man creates comfort and conducive environment for the man to work to his best in order to make his wife happy and in the process, he becomes successful and the opposite is the similarity hence if you are not keen to select a right partner, life might be difficult for you throughout and if you ever want a disorganised family is the one where there is no unity, the wife does her own things and the husband does his. In such a family, children can never be happy. More so, such a home can never develop hence you have to avoid this mistake when it is still early.

You don't have to choose 'a partner that you can live with but the one you can't live without' and to do this, many considerations are put in place. In our time, it would be our parent's responsibility to choose for us partners as we never had a choice to search for partners. Our parents would identify a home with good character and ask for their daughter, would accept to pay dearly for her and she had to be virgin for her to be accepted. In doing this, many families would reserve their character for fear and there was orderliness and hospitality in every home but now, that is history and I know it sounds weird to you for your father to choose for you a partner however you have to at least move by their principles for you to choose along lasting partner.

You have attended the same school or even met at work place but before you develop a thought, first know their full names and get to know their parents. If you have interest in them, do your background research and know how that family behaves. This will save you the last-minute embarrassment when you are already in love with them and you find they have a character you can't accommodate for example witch craft or cannibalism. After finding out more about their background, then you can feel secure around them and ask your parents, friends or relatives to continue making you any other research that you may want. If they can open up and tell you their parents, culture, then you can trust them however if they can't, keep them on a distance because you may bring them closer to you and they break your heart or you learn their weird characters.

I am telling you this at a young age my child so that you know the people you be friend, if possible where they come from, their parents so that you know their address and can easily tress them when need arises. If you know where they come from, you will be free going to that place since you know you have a friend there and you can also invest or do business in that area. I hope this message makes sense to you when you grow up and you are seriously searching for a partner.

### THE NEED FOR GOD.

My child all these topics are complicated to learn but there is a helper who can never leave you alone and can help you easily memorise every topic in this book and that is God. Life was complicated for me and had I not met God in my life, I would never have stabilised to produce you my child. When you are in school parents far away from you and teachers hard to approach, God is your only comfort. When bullies are around you, you turn to God for prayer and he listens to your prayers. In reading for an examination or starting a project its God who is always faithful answering every prayer you make to him. He is the one you tell your sorrows and are assured of privacy and help, he becomes apparent when your parents go, he is a husband to the widowed, provides to the orphans, he is the strength to the leaders, never late in answering prayers and neither is he very early, he always come at the right time when you need him and can't wait any longer.

My child, you should have your trust in God as this gives you hope and a person to believe in when need arises. There is a time when you will feel depressed at school or alone and I won't be around to comfort you my child hence unless you have God who can comfort you, life might be difficult for you. Your God knows you my child, right from the day you were born he has been with you and by your side asking you to accept him to come into your life to manage it. He sends his angels to guide you every single day so that you don't get into trouble. When you sin, he forgives you and is always welcoming when you repent and that's why you have to give time to your heavenly father. Every time you wake up, thank him for protecting you through the night and pray for a successful and productive day. In doing so, it calms you down knowing you have someone you pay your respect to, is taking care of you and can never be corrupted.

Focus on your activities and God shall bless the work of your hands. Accept to pass through difficulties because God can't give you a load you can't manage hence a reason for persisting my child as pure gold is heated first. The challenges and difficulties you face are meant to build you and not to break you. Fight harder, trust in God and you will succeed.

## THE FAMILY BOND.

My dear child, the reason I have given you all this content is mainly because I am aging and when I go, the family must keep upright and it must survive up to the next generation. I have entrusted you with all this knowledge because I see the competence in you and capability to protect my family and maintain my achievements. If you are given a responsibility my child you must take it up until you get a rightful person whom to give the responsibility.

There is no problem assuming responsibility my child, when you see anything wrong make it right however in anything you are doing, don't expect a return. Making what is wrong right strengthens your sense of judgement and decision making as it makes you alert and outstanding even in dealing with other people. This trait also wins trust from majority people since they know they are dealing with an informed person.

The family is something you can't play with had it not been my efforts to keep this family intact, you would have no relatives and no source of help or comfort hence you must protect your family since its already in your hands. It doesn't matter whether you are the first born or not, when need arises, please fill in the gap since you have the knowledge and what it takes to save the family assume the responsibility and do what is necessary.

About the author.

The author Norman is an exceptional in his field with excellent history and performance in all his academic records. Understanding life at an early age and the challenges faced by the youth, he came up with the idea to help parents advise the youth concerning all the challenges they face. This would help maintain the culture and the family lineage. Realising that the challenges of all the youth are almost the same, we base on them to come out with relevant measures how you can enjoy your life to the fullest and bring you advice that our parents got from their parents which helped them build their homes to the level where they are now. Relevant knowledge which applies to the whole world and can help maintain character in families across the globe has been extended to you and if you follow them, you will be outstanding with successful families.

The author also offers guidance and counselling to children and how to change their character so in case of any guidance, help or need of the services, you can reach out to him on:

Email: nonix743@gmail.com

Phone: +256772097812

WhatsApp: +256781771055

YouTube: Nonix Ally